<u>Yes, It's Real:</u>
<u>Hypnosis For Beginners</u>
by Chad Reinhardt

Chad Reinhardt

CONTENTS

ACKNOWLEDGEMENTS:

I'd first like to thank Rebecca, who made this book possible. I'd also like to thank everyone who has supported the series over the years, it's been a privilege to be able to explore hypnosis with all of you.

PREFACE:

As the title states this book is meant for beginners. It's written in a casual, almost conversational manner so that the concepts are a little easier to understand. Hypnosis can be such a complicated subject; it's so easy for those starting out to get overwhelmed in all the technical terms and knowledge needed to fully grasp and understand it. This book is meant to simplify a lot of those processes and principles.

When I had first started out as a hypnotist I struggled to find answers to a lot of my questions and it took years of searching and exploring to begin to put the pieces together. I've now conducted over forty hypnosis sessions through my series, Hypnosis On Display, and I wanted to share the knowledge I've accumulated and present it in a way that anyone can pick up and understand. While I hope enthusiasts will find some value in these pages as well, it is meant for the beginners trying to grasp and learn the art of hypnosis.

Hypnosis has always been a topic that fascinated me and it continues to amaze me. It had been a lifelong hope that I could find a way to show people what I found so interesting about it and hopefully help quiet that inevitable question I'm asked so often. I have tried to do that with Hypnosis On Display, but I think giving the average person the tools to learn and experience it for themselves is just as important in accomplishing this.

I hope these pages not only show the passion I have for hypnosis, but also start you on the right path in your understanding and learning of the hypnotic state.

CHAPTER 1 – HYPNOSIS AND THE HYPNOTIC STATE:

There are few topics as complicated and misunderstood as hypnosis; to this day it is still shrouded in mystery and myth. It is a tool used by therapists and psychologists, magicians and street performers, as a way of opening the subconscious mind for healing and entertainment. Through hypnosis someone can cure fears, disrupt bad patterns, or think they're a chicken.

Lately hypnosis has been taken a little more seriously by the scientific communities, but it is still largely misunderstood. This lack of proper understanding leads to a lot of confusion. One of the first questions I'm asked when I say that I am a hypnotist is, "Is it real?" It's not only a terrible question to ask a hypnotist, but it also shows just how little is known or understood about hypnosis, not only by the general public but even enthusiasts. So what is hypnosis?

Well to give you a very technical definition of hypnosis: the hypnotic state is an enhanced state of focus and relaxation where the subconscious mind is accessed, with different levels of depth a subject can be guided to. Each level provides different phenomena and experiences. Typically this state requires a heavy focus on relaxation, where the conscious mind is put into a state of heavy relaxation or sleep, while the subconscious is gradually opened up and woken.

I'm sure to many that sounds like a bunch of gibberish so I'll break things down a bit. Most people first see the hypnotic state as some form of sleep because the hypnotized subject looks as if they're sleeping, but while a hypnotic subject certainly is in a relaxed state, it is quite different from sleep. They are not dreaming; they are still in a state of awareness, listening and able to communicate. They can move, even open their eyes, while remaining completely hypnotized.

When a hypnotized subject's brain waves are measured the hypnotic state should range somewhere close to the "alpha" brain wave state, which is between your normal waking conscious "beta" waves and the light sleeping "theta" waves. A hypnotized subject is more sensitive to their surroundings than someone who is sleeping. Often their mind is aware to some extent of what's going on around them, though in the deeper levels of trance we would hope to neutralize that.

When you're attempting to hypnotize a subject, what you are really trying to do is guide their normal waking conscious mind into a state of relaxation, while at the same time gradually allowing their subconscious mind (which is the mind we're actually speaking to in trance) to become more aware and able to accept our suggestions more directly. So while it does look like they are sleeping and a part of their mind is relaxed enough to be sleeping, we are still attempting to keep part of their mind aware and at attention.

We'll go deeper into the differences between one's conscious and subconscious minds a little later as well, but for now that should be enough to help you understand what is happening during the hypnotic process.

CHAPTER 2 – THE THREE LEVELS OF TRANCE:

The hypnotic trance can be looked at in three parts, or three distinct levels that a subject can reach through hypnosis, each with its own distinct phenomena and effects. I'm sure as time goes on more levels will be added to this as we begin to understand hypnosis better, but for the time being these three levels are a helpful way of looking at things.

The first level is the light trance, which involves the subject putting their critical faculties on hold. This means they have bypassed the filter the conscious mind creates to sort through information, deciding how they respond to things or deciding how or why they might react to certain suggestions. You might get eye closure here, you might get them to raise their hand as if it's floating, or returning to trance with a trigger.

The second level is the simple trance, in which the subject shows the appearance of being in a deep trance and even responds to more complicated suggestions, but internally is merely compliant with suggestions, not fully experiencing the suggestions as their real and true reality.

The light and the simple trance can be difficult to distinguish; both appear as if the subject is in a deep trance, but their mind in these levels of trance is much more active than we are looking for in a deep trance. There is too much going on internally. The subject's mind is still processing information from the environment, both from their primary experience (sensory perception), and secondary experience (internal representations of their world and reality). In these two lighter levels of trance the subject can still experience hypnotic suggestions, and should not be considered failures at all. For some subjects it can take quite a bit of time being hypnotized and getting used to the hypnotic state before they could ever reach that final level.

That, of course, brings us to the final level and deepest hypnotic state to be achieved: the deep trance. In deep trance a subject experiences suggestions as reality; no longer processing information from their primary and secondary experience, but receiving those experiences from the hypnotic suggestions presented to them. To experience this state, most subjects will require a great deal of time spent in trance and getting used to being hypnotized, anywhere from two hours to seven or eight hours. Some subjects out there are quite special and achieve this state rapidly, but even for them I would still suggest at least an hour to two hours of being under trance to reach this state.

Now, these levels of trance are only tools and symbols to help you understand hypnosis better and I would not consider them rigid or complete, only mere guidelines of reference to help a hypnotist gauge a subject's state. Every subject is unique and some will throw these guidelines aside and leave you dumbfounded. That is what makes hypnosis so interesting.

CHAPTER 3 – THE HYPNOTIC INDUCTION:

The hypnotic induction is the process and methods used to guide a subject into the hypnotic trance. It is the doorway into the subconscious mind. It is the hypnotist's greatest tool, bar none. There are literally hundreds, if not thousands, of different hypnotic inductions and methods used to hypnotize a subject, but for now we'll split them up into two different categories to make things a little easier. Those two categories are: the Traditional Induction and the Instant Induction.

<u>The Traditional Induction</u>: The traditional induction is an induction focused on heavy relaxation. It is likely the most popular form of inducing trance, used by hypnotherapists and more serious hypnosis enthusiasts. It is the way hypnosis was originally conceived and performed by James Braid, and I believe it to be the best method of hypnotic induction to this day.

Often the hypnotist will have the subject lie down or sit somewhere comfortably and will begin speaking to them and relaxing their mind. Usually it starts with having them focus on something that will keep their attention while you speak to them, though this isn't necessarily needed.

There are hundreds of variations on this induction, but I call it traditional because it is the foundation of most hypnotists' induction, outside of stage and street performances. It should be used to begin any hypnotic process if possible.

<u>The Instant Induction</u>: The instant induction is an induction that uses focus and surprise to shock the subject into a

state of hypnosis. Typically the hypnotist will have a subject focus on something like their hand while it's moved in front of the subject's eyes or shaking the subject's hand repeatedly. Then the hypnotist introduces a sudden jolt of the subject's arm or the pulling of their head with the instruction to sleep to induce trance. This disruption breaks the pattern you previously set, creating a moment of surprise, opening the mind to the hypnotic trance. It has to be done very rapidly, with the instruction to sleep given while the subject feels the momentary sense of confusion.

It can be a powerful tool when used with the traditional induction, or it can be a quick way of inducing light trance for street or stage shows. It does require a very susceptible subject if not paired with the traditional induction, so while it is more flashy for those entertainment purposes, it's not nearly as successful and will require quite a bit of deepening from there to enter any of those deeper levels of trance. However, with a good subject it will certainly do for creating a light enough trance to have them follow some simple suggestions to wow a crowd.

While there are many ways of inducing a hypnotic trance, I use only two to make things as simple as possible to learn. I feel too many hypnotists pride themselves on how many inductions they might know, being able to quickly fire off the official names as if it means something. I can honestly say I know only a few induction names.

It's better to approach the hypnotic induction more openly. I might have the subject focus on my finger, a handshake, a spot on the wall, even the sound of something off in the distance. It all depends on the situation, and forcing yourself into the confines of an already set induction greatly limits your abilities.

CHAPTER 4 – DEEPENING THE TRANCE:

The hypnotic induction will begin the process and guide a subject into the hypnotic state, but this only takes them to the early levels of trance. If you are looking to take a subject to those deeper levels of trance it's going to require something that is referred to as "deepening".

There are many different ways to deepen a trance, perhaps just as many as there are to induce trance. Usually the hypnotist calls upon the subject's imagination and has them imagine situations that further relax them as they encourage them to go deeper and deeper into trance. One of the most popular examples of a deepener is counting down from 5 or 10, and suggesting that with each number counted the subject will go deeper into trance. However, this doesn't utilize the subject's imagination which is a very important facet of hypnotic suggestion.

The subconscious mind lives through the imagination; imagination is the language of the subconscious mind. So while simply counting down is a useful tool to help guide them deeper, it will have a much more pronounced effect if it's tied to some metaphor or imagery that the subject can use as an example of deepening.

I prefer to use what's known as the Staircase Method. I have the subject imagine they are standing at the very top of a small flight of stairs and at the bottom of those stairs is a large, comfortable bed, perhaps with some nice, cozy looking pillows. With each number you count down from 10 to 1, they can take a step further down these stairs, relaxing with each one, and when you reach the number 1 they can lie down in that bed and relax even further. This is a simple but very effective example of a deepener. You can use any sort of metaphor or imagery whether it be moving down an elevator, walking down a quiet path, rocking in a hammock, or even watching waves wash back and forth on a beach. It really doesn't matter as long as it's going to engage the subject's imagination and attention and going to help them relax.

It's also important you change up the imagery used in an induction if the subject has already been hypnotized by yourself before. The subconscious mind responds better to imagery that is new to their imagination, so if you've had them move down the stairs before in trance, it might be better to go with another image for their imagination.

I also speak to it later in the book but you should make sure you keep the subject engaged so that they don't actually fall asleep. You want the subject relaxed, but they *can* fall asleep while in trance, and we don't want that, so you have to speak in a way that keeps them engaged and interested in the process. Don't prattle on too long on an induction, deepener, or even a suggestion. If you're bored, they probably are too.

This is another reason why you shouldn't rely on scripts for an induction and improvise with your own inductions. It's pretty easy to tell when someone's reading from a script; an improvised induction feels different.

CHAPTER 5 – SIGNS OF TRANCE:

It can be difficult recognizing signs of trance in a subject and they can be quite deceiving as well. They are not always an accurate method of judging the subject's state of trance. However, they can be useful tools in helping one understand where a subject is in the process. So here are a few different signs of trance you can keep an eye out for as they move through the hypnotic induction.

<u>Heaviness in the Limbs</u>: If the hypnotist were to pick up a hypnotized subject's arm while they are in trance, a good sign that they are in deep trance is a heavy, limp hand and arm. It shows deep relaxation, but also a lack of focus and attention on holding or moving their arm. However, it's important to remember that you should mention to your subject that you are indeed about to move their body in some form, as you don't want to alert them or scare them when you do.

<u>Rapid Eye Movement</u>: Rapid eye movement or REM is a very good sign of trance and I've also found that it can be a good sign that your subject might be highly responsive and suggestive. If you look closely while they are hypnotized and their eyes are closed, it can look as if their eyes are moving about or darting around rapidly.

When I was younger I believed REM was in fact a bad sign as it seemed to me at the time that if their eyes are moving about that much they can't be relaxed and must be too focused on what I was saying. Of course, I now know REM is a big part of our natural sleep cycle during the night and there are a lot of signs that it plays a big part in the hypnotic state.

Eye-Rolling: Eye-rolling is, in my opinion, the very best sign not only of a hypnotized subject as they enter trance or even while they rest in trance, but it's also a very good sign that the subject is highly responsive and susceptible to hypnotic suggestion. If you see it in a subject, you're certainly on the right path.

You should keep in mind, however, that these aren't sure things. Sometimes these are just signs that the subject *could* be a good subject, not that they are currently in a deep trance. Sometimes the best way to find out is to simply communicate with your subject and ask them how they feel, ask them if they can go deeper. Encourage easy communication with yourself while they are in trance and use it to take them further and further into that hypnotic trance.

CHAPTER 6 – HYPNOTIC SUGGESTION:

How you present and verbalize your suggestion to the subject can be more complicated than one would presume. It likely has a greater effect than even depth of trance. You want to be direct with your suggestion and frame it in a way that's going to be as easy and simple as possible for the subject to understand. You also want to keep in mind, as I've said before, the language of the subconscious mind is the imagination, so you also want to tie all of your suggestion in with some sort of metaphor or imagery. If you can't find imagery to accompany your suggestion, and I will give an example below to help you out, I would recommend you at least have them directly imagine the suggestion or how it might feel.

It's also important to frame your suggestions with a heavy emphasis on the emotional side of the suggestion, trying to paint it in a positive light if possible. The subconscious mind is the part of you that controls and creates your moods, it lives within them, and if you can frame your suggestion in a way that emphasizes that, the subconscious is more likely to be accepted. When the subconscious is presented with two options, the stronger emotional response will likely win out.

As an example, let's say you want to make your hypnotized subject feel cold. You would not suggest to the subject directly, "You are cold". It might have some effect that way, but of course your suggestion can have much more weight behind it. I would frame it this way:

"I want you to imagine a big block of ice, a block of ice roughly the size of your body, perhaps a little larger, and as you imagine that piece of ice I want you to imagine how it might feel if your body was resting on top of that block of ice. I'm sure it's easy enough to imagine how cold that might feel on your skin, and how that cold might travel through your body. I'm sure you can imagine how cold it would be if that ice were all around your body, and how incredibly cold that you would make you feel. I want you to imagine that now, and as you do, really feel how cold that is making your body, as if that ice is moving through you, that cold travelling further and further."

This is a great example of how you should frame any of your suggestions. It puts a heavy emphasis on the imagination and has them imagine the suggestion several times, but it also creates a sort of emotional response without directly suggesting one. Additionally, it's direct about what the suggestion hopes to accomplish, and is easy for the subject to understand.

You should avoid any sort of negative suggestion or imagery at all costs. To understand a negative suggestion, the subject must consider or imagine the negative action, thus introducing it into their minds. You must be very cautious in the way that you frame every word of the hypnotic experience you're creating for the subject, not only avoiding negative suggestions but even negative words or terms.

An example of this is perhaps you are trying to suggest a subject quit smoking. You should not frame the suggestion as "You will not smoke". Frame the suggestion instead in positive and emotionally engaging terms: "You are happy to leave smoking behind, and find freedom and happiness in better health. You can have a nice refreshing glass of water instead of smoking and will find that glass of water so entirely relaxing, knowing it's helping you change your life and make you happier and healthier."

A simple example, but it serves the purpose of showing how important it is to frame suggestions in a positive light and stay away from any sort of negative terms like, "You will not."

It should also be noted that getting a subject to accept and respond to a suggestion can require a bit of trial and error. Sometimes a subject will not accept a suggestion at first because they didn't understand it. This can be due either to the way you phrased it, because they weren't in a deep enough trance for their subconscious to fully accept it, or possibly because they didn't want to follow it. There can be a number of reasons why the subject may not be responding the way you had hoped. You can try rephrasing the suggestion, or try taking them deeper and attempt the suggestion again.

The more the subject becomes used to the hypnotic state, the easier it becomes for their mind to accept hypnotic suggestions, especially with encouragement at the end of each session. Some difficult subjects might require that breakthrough session or induction before they will accept any hypnotic suggestions at all. The best advice I can give is to keep trying.

CHAPTER 7 – THE CONSCIOUS VS THE SUBCONSCIOUS:

It's important that every hypnotist has a strong understanding of what the subconscious mind is and how it differs from the conscious mind.

The conscious mind is the everyday state; it's your normal, waking state. The conscious mind controls will power, temporary memory, analytical thought process (it looks at a problem or situation and determines the best course of action), and rational thinking (why we do what we do).

The subconscious mind can be looked at as your true, uncensored self that resides behind the conscious mind. It is always there but held back in a way by your conscious mind, which seems to gain more control as you mature. The subconscious mind controls habits (practical and unintended), emotions, permanent memory, security and protection.

It may be hard for some to imagine that your subconscious mind has so much control over what you likely consider parts of yourself that feel completely in control of your conscious mind, but I'm sure many people can understand the difference by simply remembering a time you were upset over something you knew you shouldn't have been. Your conscious, rational mind was likely telling you to calm down, knowing it wasn't something you should be so upset about, but yet you still felt that raw unsettled emotion pulling at you. This is the two minds essentially vying for control, in a way that's easy for you to understand.

Recognizing the difference between the two minds will

play a major role in how you frame your suggestions, since you are giving the suggestion to the subconscious mind, not the conscious mind. You have to frame it and verbalize it in a way that the subconscious can easily understand and accept.

It can also help your subject understand if you explain to them this difference while they are in trance. If they don't understand the difference between the conscious and subconscious, they could be getting confused with your suggestions, or even the way trance works.

CHAPTER 8 – WAKING FROM TRANCE:

Waking a subject from a hypnotic trance is one of the easier aspects of hypnosis, but there are a few things to keep in mind when you do attempt to wake a hypnotized subject.

It's always a good idea before waking them that you suggest feelings of comfort as they wake, suggesting they feel refreshed after the hypnotic experience and are ready to continue on with their day. It can be a little jarring going from the hypnotic state to their normal conscious state, and any suggestions of comfort can go a long way in ensuring the overall experience was a pleasant one.

It's important to suggest that your subject wake up slowly and at their own pace. If a subject is woken too suddenly, it can lead to some side-effects like headaches. It's best you ease them out of the trance, doing so very slowly and giving them a moment afterwards to gather themselves.

As an example of a way to wake a hypnotized subject, you can say: "In a moment I'm going to count from 1 to 5 and with each number I want you to allow yourself to wake from this state more and more, so that with the number five you can feel completely awake and alert, feeling refreshed after your experience and ready to continue on with your day."

It really doesn't matter how you decide to frame it, this is only a simple example. Just try to keep in mind the subject's comfort and how unique the hypnotic experience is. It can be a little shocking for some people, especially those involved in entertainment shows.

CHAPTER 9 – THE SUBJECT IS ALWAYS THERE:

One thing a hypnotist should always keep in mind is that no matter how deep a subject is into the hypnotic state, you are always speaking to *them*. In that sense they are always aware in some way of what instructions and suggestions they are receiving and agreeing to. This might be their subconscious self, a less restricted version of themselves, but it is still 'them' with all the morals and principles they hold. This is why you cannot make someone do something they truly don't want to do while they are hypnotized; they have to agree to that suggestion in some way. Even if they forget receiving a suggestion while in trance, they still agreed to it at the time in that state.

However, a lot of hypnotists take this for granted and speak to the subject as if they are completely asleep and not listening at all. This can greatly undermine your hypnotic suggestion and can even break trance entirely, as it can disrupt their belief in your hypnotic abilities since they obviously know they are listening to you. Speak to them almost as if they were awake and actively participating in the process, guide them along the hypnotic induction, create this space for them, but always remember that they are there and need not only to be kept engaged and entertained, but also respected.

This is also why it's so important to keep the subject interested and engaged. If you don't keep their attention, if you start to bore the subject they attention may begin to wander, which can greatly disrupt hypnotic trance. They don't necessarily have to listen to your exact words, but you want to the subject still focused on being hypnotized over thinking of what they're having for dinner that day, unless of course it's your clever way of inducing trance. It might sound funny, but something relaxing and unexpected like plans later that day can be a good way of sneaking in your induction.

CHAPTER 10 – IMAGINATION IS KING:

As I have stated, imagination and imagery are the language of the subconscious mind and every suggestion that can utilize the subject's imagination should. The conscious mind is where your will power resides and it's why you feel you choose each and every action, but where the will and the imagination (your sub-conscious) conflict, the imagination always wins.

That's a surprising statement for many to wrap their heads around, as they often consider themselves so in control of their actions, but that is what makes the hypnotic experience so intense sometimes. You're hit so suddenly with the realization that your subconscious mind is not only more in control then you might expect, but that it can also be impacted by suggestion, especially when you open yourself up to it. Imagery and the use of a subject's imagination can be looked at as the key to opening and accessing that subconscious mind.

When I was a young man exploring hypnosis, I always looked at those metaphors used in inductions as silly and exaggerated. I could not understand why they were used so frequently as the root of inductions. It can cause laughter or the giggles during an induction as well. It seems so odd to have them moving down a set of stairs or rocking in a hammock, but what I didn't know and what most subjects don't know is that imagery is the very mechanism of the hypnotic suggestion. Those over the top metaphors of imagery are the core tenants of hypnosis as a whole. Your entire approach to hypnotic inductions and hypnotic suggestion should be completely melded around stirring and utilizing the subject's imagination in any and every way possible.

The more creative and new the imagery is to the subconscious mind, the stronger the hypnotic effect so don't get lazy either and go to the well with the same imagery over and over again. This is what makes hypnosis a sort of art, because those creative hypnotists are the ones that can truly shine.

CHAPTER 11 – POST-HYPNOTIC SUGGESTIONS:

The post-hypnotic suggestion is a suggestion your subject should follow after the formal hypnotic experience has ended. They are sometimes used in therapy settings as a way to encourage beneficial changes long after trance as well as for entertainment purposes, whether that's having a subject respond to a suggestion while they feel completely awake and alert, or even having them, for example, suddenly feel cold later in the day when they hear the word ice.

I'd consider the post-hypnotic suggestion to be my favorite way to explore suggestions with hypnosis when it comes to entertainment. There's nothing quite like seeing a subject respond to a suggestion they aren't expecting or don't remember.

It's not incredibly difficult to create a post-hypnotic suggestion for a subject, but you have to be very deliberate in how you word things as you may not be there to witness their reaction. Keep your wording simple. It's also important to keep in mind that post-hypnotic suggestions don't always work, as you are attempting to create some sort of reaction outside of trance. Imagery and metaphors are very important here. I'd recommend getting some sort of confirmation from your subject that they understood the suggestion, whether a vocal queue or even something as simple as having them move their finger.

You should also keep in mind the more time between the trance and when their triggered reaction will occur, the less effect the suggestion is going to have, with the exception of those few highly suggestible subjects. Re-enforcing the suggestion with repeat hypnosis sessions will help create more long-term results.

CHAPTER 12 – EXTRA TIPS AND TIDBITS:

<u>Stringing Suggestibility Tests:</u> I recommend that if you are going to use suggestibility tests, especially more than one, you should string them together in consecutive order so that each test builds off of one another. The point of the suggestibility test is to entrench the belief that there are going to be some real physical results from their hypnosis experience, that they can be moved or impacted by the power of suggestion.

I'm not the biggest fan of suggestibility tests early on, as some subjects will be eager to test any sort of power of suggestion that you might throw at them. This can work to your advantage, as it can make your suggestions even stronger once some of that will begins to bend from suggestion, but this is reliant on the subject. If the test does not work as intended, it can completely derail your hypnosis session before it's even properly begun.

I prefer if I'm going to use them at all to at least use them after a lengthy induction so that even if they fail one of the tests you can at least bring the subject back into a relaxed trance. It's something they've already experienced and know works.
It can also help to present your suggestibility test as an experiment, and that it's perfectly okay if they fail. That way it doesn't diminish their belief in your trance completely.

<u>The Yes Set Principle</u>: Once you have someone agree with you three or four times, they are more likely to accept or agree with whatever statement or suggestion that follows. The mind gets into that groove of acceptance and once on it, it's much eas-

ier for your mind to continue with that route over taking a detour. This is a powerful tool for a hypnotist as it can be used not only in suggestibility tests as a way to increase the subject's belief in the power of suggestion and your ability as a hypnotist, but it can also be used during inductions to help build that relaxation and trance state.

As an example, during an induction you might ask the subject if they are feeling relaxed, if your words are helping them relax, and can they agree that becoming relaxed is a form of being hypnotized, so they can agree that they are being hypnotized. This sort of stringing together leading questions is a great way to help ease them into the induction not only through your suggestion, but by also helping them feel as if they are creating the experience themselves. They feel they agree with your suggestions and are not merely compliant, an important and helpful distinction. This is only a simple example though and there are countless ways the Yes Set Principle can be used by the hypnotist.

<u>Attach Emotional Responses to Suggestions</u>: When you think of the subconscious mind, you really have to remember it is quite different from the normal, conscious mind. The subconscious mind not only speaks in the language of imagination and imagery, but is also very attached to emotions and emotional responses.

In fact, your subconscious mind is entirely in control of your emotions. This is something some people find surprising, because they likely feel in control of their emotions, but your conscious mind is only in control of how you respond to those emotions, it is the subconscious mind that brings them about and controls them. It lives within your wild emotions and that is why when you speak or suggest things to the subconscious mind, it often responds so much better to those suggestions tethered or attached to some sort of emotional response.

Some simple examples might be that they feel happy to enter hypnosis, they enjoy the feeling of comfort and warmth they feel when being hypnotized, and they can quit smoking because they know they will be much happier without that habit and free to explore that freedom and happiness they get from quitting the habit. Again, these are quick, basic examples that should help you understand the importance of framing suggestions around some emotional response.

It gives the subconscious mind that extra incentive to follow your suggestion. The strongest emotional option will win out when it comes to suggestions, so it's important to really emphasize the importance and emotional benefit they might experience from your suggestions.

<u>Authority Principle</u>: Suggestions or statements become more acceptable or believable when they are coming from an authority figure like a hypnotist. When you can create that sense of authority and confidence before your subject, it makes your suggestions much more pronounced. You must not only believe in your suggestions, but you must believe in yourself and present everything with a strong air of confidence.

If a suggestion fails or they are taking to a hypnotic induction slower than expected, do not show worry or distress. It's only going to erode your sense of authority in the situation and give them the upper hand. You must always roll with the experience and present suggestions as experiments, or at the very least make sure they understand that just because they do not follow one suggestion or another that doesn't mean they aren't hypnotized or won't follow any suggestions at all. Every subject is unique and will experience things quite differently.

The authority principle is also a key reason why hypnosis can sometimes fail early on with a subject that you are close with, as they may not be able to see you as that authority figure at first due to whatever history you might have with them. It's important to remember this and try to plan for it if you are hypnotizing someone you know on that personal level. Perhaps create the air of authority well before the hypnotic experience is set to happen.

<u>The Principle of Repetition</u>: Repetition is a very important key when it comes to hypnotic suggestion. It is one of the most important tools a hypnotist can utilize, though it is suggested you keep your repetition creative so that you don't completely

bore the subject's subconscious mind.

The Hypnotic Triple Rule is that you repeat every important suggestion or instruction at least three times to accumulate the effect. I would suggest going even further than that, but again, try to keep each repetition a little fresh and different to help keep that creative subconscious mind engaged in your suggestions and words.

<u>Compliment Your Subject</u>: It is important to always compliment your subject and assure them as you go through every step of the process that they are doing very well and are following all of your suggestions as they should be. Doubts the subject might have about whether they are following along or experiencing everything as they should be can greatly disrupt the process. Often a subject will not communicate this to you properly as the experience is happening, so you should always be assuring them that they are doing perfectly well. You can even suggest that they will experience things in their own way to help cover you if they interpret your suggestions or instructions differently than expected.

<u>Belief and Hypnotic Suggestion</u>: It is a conventional belief among hypnotists that a subject will not actualize hypnotic behaviour or follow a suggestion the hypnotist does not believe possible or capable of actually happening. Now I'm hesitant to add this as I do not believe it is quite accurate. It's important not to expect any results at all, but go with the flow of the experience and what the subject presents you. It is also very important that you have a strong belief in what you are doing and both your capabilities as a hypnotist and the subject's capabilities under hypnotic trance. There is more information being sent to a subject than simple words moving across a room, some forms of information I'm sure we're not even aware of, and so it's important even in your own mind to keep that positive, confident attitude and to always project that and present that to the subject in front of you.

<u>Confusion</u>: A state of confusion can be a helpful tool for the hypnotist. When you can create a true sense of confusion inside the subject's mind, they will leap at the first sense of clarity that

is presented to them, and if you're doing things right that first moment of clarity will be your hypnotic suggestion. It also causes a subject's attention to focus inward instead of outward towards the hypnotist's words and actions. This can help deepen a trance for those who find their mind wandering.

Now that is not to say your main goal with every induction should be to confuse your subject, but if you have a subject who is struggling to enter a hypnotic state using an induction that emphasizes and attempts to create a sense of confusion can be a way of showing them the door to the subconscious mind.

Confusion is also often a helpful tool when it comes to the instant induction. That sense of confusion a subject can feel as they are waiting to see what you are going to do is the very way of creating trance. Move your hand one way and have them focus on it while you start counting at random, and then suddenly pull their hand and command them to sleep. This is a simple way of creating an instant hypnotic induction. It would require a great deal of hypnotic deepening to follow if you were hoping to bring them into these deeper levels of trance, but it is a way of creating that first step and bypassing their critical faculties.

<u>Keep Expectations in Check</u>: It is important to keep any expectations you might have regarding the hypnosis session in check, as hypnosis provides a unique experience for every subject and often a hypnosis session is going to take turns that you weren't expecting. When this happens, if you were too set on a set of circumstances happening, if you expect a suggestion to work in a particular way and it doesn't, you can often be left scrambling and a subject can pick this up very quickly. It can result in terminating trance or at the very least throwing their attention off and in other directions.

The best way to approach a session is to be excited about each and every turn that might take place. Be curious about what might take place, but don't allow yourself to fall into a line of thinking that hypnosis absolutely will happen and it will happen the way you expect. Some hypnotists or teachers recommend extreme confidence and while it is important to be confident about yourself and your own abilities, it is not wise to be confident in expectations. Everyone can be hypnotized, but many can and will struggle.

Expect the unexpected and try to enjoy that aspect as much as you can. Revel in the challenge, but do not allow your confidence to betray you. Once you lose a subject's confidence it will be difficult to gain it back.

<u>Amnesia and Trance</u>: As I've stated earlier, imagination is a key component of the hypnotic trance and hypnosis itself. It's often desirable for a hypnotist to create a sense of amnesia for a subject, especially in an entertainment or stage setting where having a subject forget something that just happened or having them forget a trigger they will soon respond to only adds to the level of entertainment and wonder.

An important way of creating this state of amnesia is with the imagination, and in particular I've found encouraging them to imagine their memories or thoughts you want them to forget like dreams they have during their sleep at night. They can remember how difficult it can be to remember those dreams as they become more aware and alert in the morning. They can look at these memories or thoughts like those dreams in the morning, and as they awaken from the trance they can find those thoughts drifting away, becoming more and more difficult to remember as they become more and more alert, feeling refreshed and awake.

This is another simple example, but a powerful one at creating amnesia as it is an idea or metaphor that everyone should be familiar with in some way. That is the importance of hypnotic suggestion, using their imagination and imagery they are actually familiar with or can understand. If it's outside their own imagination it won't work as intended. Frame suggestions or imagery in a way that is catered towards each individual and their own experiences.

<u>Distinctions Between State and Awake</u>: It is important that as you give suggestions and get your subject familiar with the hypnotic state, you make clear distinctions between the hypnotic state and their normal waking state. This not only makes it

easier to introduce post-hypnotic suggestions, but it also further encourages their belief in their current hypnotic state, perhaps allowing them to go deeper.

Hypnosis is a mutual experience and having them actually believe they are hypnotized is an important tool for a hypnotist. When you make that distinction between the hypnotic state and their waking state, especially if you can get them to confirm they are in a different state, any at all, it further solidifies any suggestions that will follow.

<u>Induction Length:</u> Longer inductions (at least ten minutes in length) are far more effective in creating a hypnotic state. That isn't to say instant inductions can't be useful for a hypnotist, but they are better used as a back-up or a deepener following a traditional induction using some form of attention and eye fixation. Milton Erickson believed it required closer to seven or eight hours of trance experience to create a deep level of trance, though at the very least an hour, and that's much closer to what I believe myself.

While long inductions can allow a subject's mind to wander, they can be incredibly effective at creating deep levels of trance for new subjects. However, this requires a hypnotist talented enough to keep their attention somewhat fixed as they are guided deeper and deeper. If you are not too confident in your own creative abilities, pick a pre-written induction like the walkthrough provided near the end of the book and take them through it. Wake them up and follow it with another pre-written induction (a different one from the first) and continue with deepening. This repeating of inductions over and further deepening is a bit of a shortcut for those who require it, though it's much better a hypnotist keeps them in that relaxed state as long as possible as they take the subject deeper. It allows much more immersion into the relaxation, but again only take this path if you are very comfortable and familiar with the inductions and can keep a healthy pace and rhythm to what you are saying.

<u>Cold Control Theory:</u> I found that the cold control theory was a helpful way of looking at hypnotic suggestions when you

are initially trying to wrap your head around the mechanisms at work in the hypnotized mind.

It's believed that hypnosis bypasses a subject's intent. They don't fully realize or understand why they are doing something, they are simply doing it. If the subject intended on raising their arm, the arm would rise, but if the subject is unaware of the intention or unaware they intended to raise their arm the arm would appear to rise completely on its own.

That is precisely what the hypnotized subject experiences. They find themselves doing things, often silly things in an entertainment or stage setting, but they are unaware they intended to do these things or agreed to do them while under hypnosis so they appear to have lost control of their will.

However, in deeper states of hypnosis this can change a little as a subject in a deep level of trance can have their entire reality altered and believe or see things differently from how they really are.

<u>Rapport and Belief:</u> Creating a stronger belief in hypnosis with a subject can be a helpful tool in fostering the hypnotic trance, especially if it's done prior to the formal hypnosis session. A good way of doing this is to simply have a short chat with your subject about what they believe regarding hypnosis and or what will happen to them while they are hypnotized. This way if they have any pre-conceived notions regarding hypnosis, and they are a lot of them out there, you can quickly dismiss these ideas which would only become hurdles for you later on during the induction. It's also a great way of building rapport and trust with a subject which is also very important.

<u>Body Movements in Trance:</u> Sometimes something as simple as moving a subject's hand up and down during an induction can be a powerful tool in creating those deeper states of hypnosis. It's a technique that has been used for many years and I've found it best used with those difficult subjects who have trouble concentrating or during instant inductions to help guide them deeper a little more quickly.

I imagine one of the main mechanisms of this method is

that it engages the subject's attention and focus with movement, allowing the hypnotist's words to kind of slip past their critical faculties and into their subconscious mind more readily. Sometimes instead of moving one's hand, a hypnotist can work the subject's body back and forth or in circles, as well as rocking or spinning the subject's head.

Almost any body part will do as long as you keep their attention focused on that motion and relax them further or surprise them with a sudden jerk or drop to take them deeper.

<u>New Metaphors and Imagery:</u> Unconventional imagery or metaphors are processed by the same side of your brain that is active during hypnosis, suggesting metaphors or imagery the mind isn't used to can help hypnotic suggestion. This really highlights the artistry in the hypnotic induction and the hypnotist himself as it takes an artist or a creative mind to produce these unconventional approaches to the hypnotic induction. You must always keep the mind not only engaged, but challenged. You can't go to the well over and over again with the same subject, reusing the same images and metaphors and expect them to have the same, renewed effect.

This is why I encourage hypnotists not to focus so much on silly terms and names for different inductions, memorizing these rigid methods of induction and instead focus on improvised approaches to engaging and relaxing a subject's mind. There are hundreds of ways you can approach the hypnotic induction as long as you relax and focus a subject's mind. Those guidelines leave a tremendous amount of room for improvisation and creativity and that's an element that must be embraced by the hypnotist if they truly want to master the art.

I would recommend reading through the induction walkthrough in the next chapter and challenge yourself by writing your own version in your own vocabulary. This is how you should approach every induction and it's a good method to get you used to thinking for yourself.

CHAPTER 13 – HYPNOTIC INDUCTIONS (FURTHER EXPLANATION):

Since the hypnotic induction is going to be your most important tool as a hypnotist, I wanted to expand further and perhaps dispel some assumptions or bad tendencies.

It's easy to look at the instant induction as being more desirable than the traditional induction since it's not only quicker, but it lends itself to the more fantastical part of hypnosis and the imagination. However, alone the instant induction is not going to be capable of creating a deep state of hypnosis. You cannot snap your fingers and tell a subject to sleep, and then expect them to actually respond to even basic hypnotic suggestions. It's not going to happen without some acting on the part of your subject.

The instant induction can be effective as a way to start your hypnosis session, especially in an entertainment setting, but it needs more. If you continue with several instant inductions, after three or four you will begin to see some success with your hypnotic suggestions, but you should not be giving any suggestions (outside of further relaxation and deepening) until at least three consecutive instant inductions have been performed. This is just a general rule of thumb, but an excellent guideline when it comes to the instant induction.

Even with several consecutive instant inductions, you'll likely only be able to get some responses to basic hypnotic suggestions. I've been able to hypnotize subjects to follow some pretty wild hypnotic suggestions, but in order to do some of the more extreme things I've captured on film, it required anywhere from an hour to three working with the subject in trance and getting them accustomed to following hypnotic suggestions.

With all that said, I always recommend a hypnotist focus on the traditional induction as their main way of inducing trance, especially to start a hypnosis session. There's something very powerful in relaxation and the way it relates to your subconscious mind. It opens the mind to suggestion in a way that an instant induction cannot easily replicate. It is by far the most effective way to create a deep trance.

The traditional induction is often taught with some form of having the subject close their eyes through relaxation and focus. This eye-closure by the subject through your suggestion helps solidify belief in hypnosis and your abilities as a hypnotist, but it can also offer challenges. If a subject really wants to they can keep their eyes open even with your suggestion, and some will take this opportunity as a way to defy you as a hypnotist and authority figure.

If you cannot get them to close their eyes during the induction, you can count them down and suggest when you reach the number one you want them to close their eyes and relax, then continue on with your induction. This won't work with those especially stubborn subjects though, as they'll need some sort of confirmation that hypnotic suggestion can have an effect on them. The best way to deal with this is go through several different inductions, each followed by further relaxation.

As an example, if you have the subject focus on a candle and can't get their eyes to close, suggest they close them at your count and then go through a simple deepener like walking down a staircase and relaxing. From there you can have them open their eyes again, and then have them focus on a pocket watch instead and again try to get eye-closure. Just follow this cycle over and over again until you start to see the subject break. You will eventually begin to see a change in their demeanor as they realize their defiance does not mean the end of your hypnosis session.

Of course, you do not need to go through eye-closure while

performing a traditional induction in order to hypnotize a subject. You can start with them closing their eyes, and from there begin to relax their mind and deepen the hypnotic state. Eye-closure is preferred since it can produce a deeper trance quicker, but I don't recommend this approach with a subject you know is likely to resist or defy you as a hypnotist. The best way to gauge a subject before your hypnosis session is talking with them and getting to know them, but for some you'll have to find this out the hard way.

It should also be said that the best induction method isn't one or the other, but the both of them used together. As a pair, they create a powerful set of tools for the hypnotist. I only recommend the traditional induction be used to *start* the hypnotic process; the instant induction is an excellent way of returning a subject to trance during a session after waking them for feedback or to follow a suggestion.

CHAPTER 14 – TRADITIONAL INDUCTION WALKTHROUGH:

Before you begin the traditional induction you want to have your subject either sit or lie in a comfortable position that they can remain in for 15 to 20 minutes at least. I prefer to have the subject lying down since you don't need to worry about their neck or head needing readjusting, a distraction that can come up when the subject is sitting.

Have the subject place their hands at their sides, not crossed, as a way of making sure they'll be comfortable but also creating a sense of authority early on. Ask them if that feels comfortable, if they can hear you, and then ask them if they'll be able to relax. If you get a yes three times, you've created that yes set principle.

You can then say to them, "I'm sure as you get a little more comfortable, you can already feel yourself beginning to relax more. Can you feel that?"

You've already set them up to create an easy yes and create that relaxation in their own mind. From there you want to continue to foster that sense of relaxation for them.

"Now to help you to relax a little further we're going to do a breathing exercise. I want you to close your eyes for the next little while and I want you to really focus on your breathing. Try to notice each and every breath as you begin to relax. I want you to imagine your lungs, try to see them in your mind and as you feel them fill up with air, and deflate. I want to you allow yourself to relax more and more. Each time they open, and close, relaxing a little more."

You want to try to time when you say, "open and close" or "fill up with air and deflate" with the pace of their actual breathing, speaking very slowly and rhythmically. Remember, it's all about relaxation here.

"Now take a nice deep breath in, filling your lungs up with air, and exhale as you feel more and more of that relaxation. Do it again for me, filling your lungs up with air, and exhale as you relax more and more, deeper and deeper. Again, filling your lungs up with air, and exhale as you relax even more, feeling so heavy and comfortable. As you continue to focus on your breathing, taking nice deep breaths in and out, feel that relaxation growing stronger and stronger, as you feel yourself going deeper and deeper into that nice warm feeling."

"This is how it feels to be hypnotized; all you have to do is allow yourself to relax more and more as you listen to my voice and drift. Take another deep breath for me, filling your lungs up with air, and exhale as you relax more and more, going deeper and deeper. It feels better and better each time you take another breath in and out, relaxing more and more."

The next step depends entirely on your approach. I like to have the subject focus on a candle or a spot on the roof directly above them. For this example, we'll pretend our subject is stretched out, looking at a candle.

"You can open your eyes now and I want you to focus on the candle next to you. That's right, focus all your attention on the candle or, more specifically, the flame. Try to notice everything that you can about the flame. Perhaps you notice the way it moves and dances on the wick. Maybe you notice the colour of the flame and the way it ever so slightly changes colour. Perhaps it's something else that catches your attention and holds it, but whatever it might be I want you to continue to focus on the flame, and as you do I want you to begin to notice a warm, relaxing feeling and sensation growing in your body, starting in your lungs. As you continue to breathe in and out, relaxing more and more, watching the flame, you can feel that relaxation in your lungs growing, and with each breath it spreads out into the rest of your body."

"For now I want you to really notice that warmth and relaxation in those tiny, tiny muscles in your eyelids. The longer you watch that candle and feel its warmth the more you can feel those eyelids beginning to relax and sink, as if that warm heavy sensation is spreading through those eyelids and into your eyes. The longer you watch the candle, the more you feel those eyelids growing heavier and heavier, heavier and heavier, as if they wanted to slowly close down and allow you to relax more and more."

Keep in mind you want to keep your voice low and soft, speaking slower as the induction progresses. I like to sometimes hasten my voice a bit and then it slow again; these sporadic changes can help keep the subject focused on the induction and the process.

Their eyes might close at anytime during this part of the induction and if that does happen, just skip ahead onto the next part of the induction.

"Continue to focus on the flame as those eyes grow heavier and heavier, and I want you to imagine attached to those eyelids are two heavy lead weights. As you focus on the candle, you can feel those weights pulling and tugging on your eyelids, as they slowly close, slowly close, slowly closing, drifting down more and more, heavier and heavier."

You can continue with these sorts of suggestions and comments until you get the subject's eyes to close completely. Some subjects may require longer than others, and some may not close from this method on their own at all.

If that does happen, suggest that they get heavier as you count from 5 to 1, and when you reach the number 1 they can close them down all the way. This doesn't bypass their critical faculties because they've closed them wilfully, not from hypnotic suggestion, so you have to change your method here and try another induction. You can have them close their eyes each time you count from 5 to 1, and each time they open again it becomes harder and harder. This way you should eventually get them to keep their eyes closed from hypnotic suggestion.

For those who did get eye-closure from this method, you now want to ease them into a deeper and deeper level of trance, encouraging them to drift and experience the relaxation as they do.

"You can allow your eyes to remain closed for the time being. All you do to now is relax and drift in this comfortable, peaceful state. As you continue to drift I'm going to help you relax further and further, because even though you feel so relaxed now, you can feel even more relaxed and go even deeper into this state."

From here I like to move onto relaxing their body further and begin to engage their imagination a bit more.

"I'm going to begin relaxing you further by having you focus on different parts of your body, and we're going to allow those body parts to relax more and more. As we focus on each part of your body, I want you to do your best to imagine that body part and allow it to relax."

"We'll start with the very top of your head, and as you begin to imagine and see it in your mind, I want you to notice a slight tingle, the beginnings of a relaxing sensation that is growing stronger and stronger in the top of your head. I want you to really feel it now and I want you to let the top of your head relax."

"We're going to let that relaxation move down now as it continues to get stronger and stronger, moving from the top of your head down into your forehead and your eyebrows. As those muscles and the bones beneath them relax more and more, that sensation is getting stronger as you relax further."

"From your eyebrows and forehead, feel it move down into your eyes and those tiny, tiny muscles in your eyelids, relaxing them more and allowing your eyes to sink down a little further as you relax deeper. From your eyes you can feel it move down through your nose and cheeks, into your jaw and your mouth, as they become heavier and heavier, relaxing more and more."

"From your mouth and head you can feel that relaxing sensation move down even further into your neck, relaxing those muscles more and more. You can feel your neck getting so heavy, so heavy as it sinks into that warmth and relaxation. From your neck, you can allow it to sink into your shoulders, soaking into those muscles as your shoulders relax more, feeling the ease and peace of that relaxation."

"From your shoulders you can let it move down now into your arms, both of your arms, releasing those heavy muscles and letting them relax further. Moving through your arm, it passes through your elbows, further down, all the way to your wrists. It moves further, into your hands, right down into the very tips of your fingers."

"From your arms and shoulders you can feel it moving even further as that sensation relaxes you more and more, and you can really feel it now as it moves down into your chest and your lungs. As it does you can feel your breathing begin to slow more and more; each breath now passing that relaxation further down, allowing you to go deeper and deeper into the warmth."

"From your chest and lungs you can feel it move down into your stomach, and you can let your stomach relax. From your stomach you can feel it move down into your waist, allowing your waist to relax more and more. From your waist you can feel it move down into your thighs, soaking into those muscles as they grow heavier and heavier. From your thighs that relaxation moves down into your knees. From your knees you can feel it move down into calves. From those calf muscles, you can feel it move down into your ankles. From your ankles you can feel it move down into your feet, sinking into the soles of your feet, moving all the way down into the very tips of toes."

"Your whole body can feel that relaxation now, and I want you to allow a wave of relaxation to move down from the top of your head all the way to the tips of your toes, that's right, relaxing your entire body more and more. You can do it again and feel that get stronger, feeling that wave pass through you. You can do it one more time, that wave passing over you, helping you sink a little deeper, going a little further into that warmth."

"As we go along, just allow yourself to soak in that relaxation, drifting in this peaceful, comfortable place."

Now that their body should be sufficiently relaxed, we want to move onto relaxing their mind and allowing that conscious mind to sink into a relaxed sleep, while we slowly open the subconscious mind more and more. The next step is a classic deepener that engages their imagination.

"In this relaxed state, your imagination is much stronger than it normally would be, capable of all kinds of powerful things. I'm going to have you use your imagination now and I want you to imagine you're lying in a comfortable bed, but this isn't just any bed. This bed is in an elevator, an elevator all the way up on the 20th floor of an office building. We're going to take the elevator from that 20th floor, all the way down to the 1st floor, and as we do all you have to do is lie in that bed and relax more and more with each floor we reach."

"We'll start with the 20th floor and as we do I want you to feel that elevator begin to move and drop, and you can feel your body moving down with it, sinking, taking you deeper and deeper as you get closer to that next floor. As we reach that next floor, you can let yourself relax even more. Feel it now as we reach the 19th floor. Already you can feel yourself getting heavier with that new floor, a little more relaxed, but that elevator continues to move again as it takes you further down."

"I want you to feel that relaxation growing more and more as you feel us reach the 18th floor, heavier and heavier, but the elevator continues down again from the 18th floor, down, heavier and heavier, to the 17th floor. You can feel that relaxation growing stronger now, deeper and deeper into that warmth, but the elevator moves again, pulling again on your body as it takes you deeper. From the 17th floor you can feel that heaviness so intensely as we reach the 16th floor. Relaxing more and more, the elevator continues down again, your body sinking with it, deeper and deeper as we reach the 15th floor."

"You can feel that heaviness growing as we go deeper down and you can feel that relaxation grow as we reach the 14th floor. It almost feels as if there were magnets on the bottom of the elevator, those magnets pulling down on your body, pulling down on your muscles, pulling you further and further into that bed as you relax more and more, but the elevator continues to drop again."

"Moving from the 14th floor, you can allow yourself to go deeper and deeper as we reach the 13th floor. It feels so heavy to settle on this floor, as you relax more and more, but the elevator moves again. From the 13th floor it moves down deeper to the 12th floor. So heavy and so relaxed as it moves again from the 12th floor down to the 11th floor. You can feel that relaxation more and more, but it moves again, taking you deeper, from the 11th floor all the way down to the 10th floor."

"It's so easy to relax and sink further into that bed as the elevator moves again from the 10th floor down to the 9th floor; so heavy and so relaxed, as it takes you deeper. From the 9th floor it moves again, deeper and deeper, the relaxation growing as you reach the 8th floor. It moves again, deeper, as you go from the 8th floor, heavier and heavier, down to the 7th floor. From the 7th floor it sinks again, that relaxation growing, as you sink to the 6th floor. Deeper and deeper, you move from the 6th floor down the 5th floor."

"You're getting so close to a much deeper, more relaxed sleep and when we reach that number one floor you can relax all the way down, sinking deeper into that bed. Feel the elevator move again from the 5th floor, deeper and deeper, down to the 4th floor. From the fourth floor it pulls again, pulling your body deeper, heavier and heavier, as you reach the 3rd floor. From the 3rd floor it moves again, deeper and deeper, so close, so heavy, as you move down to the 2nd floor."

You'll want to count the last three numbers over again, really emphasizing each one this time, and as you reach the number one floor, really pushing that deeper relaxation with your voice.

"On the next number you can allow yourself to sink so much deeper into that bed and relax more completely. The 3rd floor, deeper and deeper, the 2nd floor, so heavy and so relaxed; and the 1st floor, sinking right down into that bed; dropping further down. You can feel yourself relaxing more and more, allowing yourself to drift and enjoy this peaceful, warm place."

You'll now want to give their subconscious mind some encouragement to open up more to your suggestions, as the conscious mind continues to drift and relax in the hypnotic state.

"All you have to do now is relax and drift in that bed, going deeper and deeper when you need to, but it's so easy just to let yourself sink in the peace and ease that you feel here. Your subconscious mind knows how to listen to any suggestions it might need in this relaxed state, all you have to do is drift and relax more and more, heavier and heavier, as you drift a little further down."

"In this state, as you relax more and more, your subconscious mind can be given suggestions or instructions to follow, and as your subconscious listens to these instructions you can just relax and sink deeper, drifting as you will. I'm going to give the subconscious mind some of those instructions now..."

From here you can move onto your first hypnotic suggestions, or you can continue with some counting down, encouraging them to go deeper with each number. You can also offer some more imagery to deepen the trance. It's really up to you; this was only to get your subject started on that hypnotic process.

CHAPTER 15 – INSTANT INDUCTION WALKTHROUGH:

The instant induction is a lot less verbal than the traditional induction, and relies a lot more on physical actions to capture the subject's attention while you lull or surprise them into a hypnotic state. There are hundreds of variations of the instant induction, but I'll go through a few examples to give you something to work with.

You should also keep in mind that typically I use an instant induction after I've put a subject through a traditional induction, and have suggested to them they'll find it very easy to return to trance. That's why they work so well in a lot of my videos, but if they aren't paired with the traditional induction, they may not be as easy as I've made it look.

The first example I'll take you through is often referred to as a handshake induction, and it's one of the more popular instant inductions out there. The concept is quite simple. You'll need to take the subject's hand in yours as if you were doing a typical handshake, making this induction a good one if you're looking to surprise your subject.

As you raise your hands up and down you'll want to suggest the subject begins to feel relaxed.

"As you feel your hand go up and down, I want you to begin to notice yourself relaxing each time, especially in those tiny, tiny muscles in your eyelids."

Each time you mention their eyes you can slow the handshake as well, just to add a non-verbal form of suggestion to the induction as well.

"Heavier and heavier, it almost feels as if there were heavy weights attached to those eyelids, and as you feel your hand go up and down, it feels as if that weight is getting heavier and heavier, as if that weight were pulling on your eyelids more and more."

You'll want to time the next sentence so that you say it just as their eyes blink or begin to close down.

"That's right, feel how heavy those eyes are becoming, slowly closing down, slowly closing down, slowly closing down."

Again this next sentence you should time it so that you're saying it just as their eyes begin to close down again.

"And you notice as your eyes close down how good it feels to close them, each time they close you can notice how easy it is to keep them closed and relax, feeling heavier and heavier with that relaxation."

Now you can repeat these heavier sort of suggestions until you eventually get them to close their eyes down. If you're struggling to get them closed, you can follow the method I went over in Chapter 13.

Once their eyes do close, you'll want to move on to a deepener that utilizes their imagination, like walking down a flight of stairs and relaxing more with each step down.

There are non verbal ways of doing this induction as well. All you need to do is secure eye-contact and slowly and deliberately begin closing your eyes as if you yourself were going into trance while you continue to shake your hands. If you continue to do this, the subject should eventually close their eyes, and you can slow the handshake each time you see them close their eyes. This subtle induction and form of suggestion can be used in a lot of different variations of the instant induction.

Another instant induction example I'll go over that I like to use is the finger-to-forehead induction. In this induction you'll want to have your subject lift their hand up so that it's at their eye level, with their their index finger pointed towards their forehead. What you're going to do is have them focus entirely on that finger while you suggest it's being pulled towards their forehead.

You can start by saying, "Now I want you to focus very closely on your finger, focus all your attention on that finger, and while you do I want you to notice that finger is actually being pulled towards your forehead. You can imagine it like a magnet in the tip of that finger, and another in your forehead, and the more you concentrate, the more you focus, the more you're going to feel that pull."

Now you have to watch carefully with this induction, because some subjects may not move their hand very quickly at all, while some will find their hand being drawn in with very little effort at all. If it's already moving, you can skip the next few sentences and move to the end of this induction.

"While you watch that finger, notice how relaxing it feels as it pulls closer. Notice how heavy it makes you feel as it moves closer and closer to your forehead. Notice how easy it is to close your eyes while it pulls, more and more."

You'll want to continue suggesting the finger moves closer and closer. When you begin to see their eyes get heavy, or the finger gets close to their forehead, you can begin with the next sentence.

"Soon your finger will touch your forehead, and when it does you'll finally be able to close your eyes completely down and relax. You'll be able to let that heaviness wash over you, and you can already feel as it as it pulls more and more, getting so close to that relaxation."

You have two options when it comes to finishing this induction. You can let the subject's finger touch their forehead, and as it does place your hand on their shoulder with the suggestion to sleep. I prefer to wait until it looks like their finger is about to touch their forehead, and then with my hand suddenly push it the remaining distance towards their forehead, while my other hand holds the back of their hand and guides it down, suggesting they sleep. This way it adds a bit more surprise to the induction and might catch them off-guard.

These two examples are simple but effective inductions to get you started, but they should be used as guidelines, not rigid scripts to be followed word for word. Let each situation dictate how you approach the hypnotic induction, because every subject is different and will present their own unique set of challenges.

CHAPTER 16 – ETHICS AND RESPONSIBILITY:

As a hypnotist it's your responsibility to care for your subject and to make sure you always treat their subconscious mind ethically and responsibly. While a subject will not accept a suggestion it is not comfortable with, you still have to make sure that your subject is always comfortable with the content of the hypnosis session, and that there is no lasting damage from the hypnosis session. You have been entrusted with their subconscious mind, and you should treat it with the care that it deserves.

Since the subconscious mind is linked so closely to a subject's emotions, it can be surprisingly easy to stir up negative emotions in a subject if you aren't careful with your wording and phrasing. Especially when you have a subject recalling any moments from the past, I'd recommend you have a strong understanding of your subject and their history, and even with that understanding a subject can still have repressed memories.

Always be sure to clear any triggers or post-hypnotic suggestions before ending a trance, unless they are meant to carry on afterwards. I've always believed that the subconscious mind is very good at recognizing when to let a suggestion go and even when it's necessary to respond to it, but you still want to be careful and make sure all suggestions have been released; not only for their safety, but for liability reasons for yourself as a hypnotist.

www.ingramcontent.com/pod-product-compliance
Lightning Source LLC
Chambersburg PA
CBHW032130050726
47590CB00008B/3033